The Inventory
by Flo Vasquez

Copyright © 2025 Flo Vasquez All rights reserved.

Scripture quotations marked NKJV are taken from

the New King James Version®.
Copyright © 1982 by Thomas Nelson.
Used by permission. All rights reserved.

Table of Contents

1. In His Presence Throughout the Day.................. 1
2. Two-edged Sword.. 3
3. As a Man Thinketh.. 5
4. A Soldier's Prayer... 7
5. Time Management.. 8
6. The Luring Wolf... 10
7. Let Go... 12
8. Fear Destroys... 14
9. Inventory Your Spiritual Walk.......................... 16
10. Your Identity in Christ..................................... 18
11. The Enemy Waits... 20
12. Don't Throw in the Towel............................... 22
13. Turn off the Phone.. 24
14. Lack of Discipline.. 26
15. Affective Prayer with the Word..................... 28
16. A Compass... 30
17. Times of Frustration....................................... 32
18. Financial Inventory... 34
19. Grace.. 36
Inventory Page... 38
20. Dirt or Diamonds.. 39
21. The Foundation of Love................................. 41
22. Clogged Heart.. 43
23. In All Things Give Thanks............................... 45
Scripture Reference List...................................... 46
Author Page.. 51

Dedication

To my beloved wife, **Leslie Vasquez-** Your love, patience, and unwavering faith have been the anchor of my journey.

This book would not exist without your prayers, encouragement, and the countless quiet sacrifices you've made along the way.

To my family, who have stood beside me through seasons of both diamonds and dirt, thank you for reminding me that God's grace is always enough.

And to every reader who opens these pages:

May you find courage to take inventory of your own life, discover the treasures hidden in your trials, and trust the One who restores all things.

-Flo Vasquez

Introduction to The Inventory

Life leaves us with an inventory: memories, wounds, lessons, and blessings. Too often, the weight of the past keeps us from stepping into the freedom God has prepared. The Inventory by Flo Vasquez is a guide to healing – a journey of faith that helps us release what no longer serves us and embrace the grace that carries us forward.

Thisbook invites readers to lay down burdens, confront the pain of yesterday, and discover the power of God's restoration. Through reflection and testimony, it shows that healing is not only possible but promised to those who trust in the Lord.

The Inventory is more than a record; it is a call to renewal. It dares us to share our stories, to walk in forgiveness, and to move boldly into the future God has designed. In these pages, Flo Vasquez offers a path toward wholeness – a reminder that in Christ, every broken piece can be made new.

1. In His Presence Throughout the Day

I want to encourage men to be aware of His presence throughout the day. David had 288 people on his praise team, thirty-seven people on his staff, seven wives and yet he still praised the Lord seven times a day. As Psalm 119:164 declares, "Seven times a day I praise You, because Your righteous judgments." (NKJV)

You can be fishing and be aware of His presence. You can be cutting the grass and be aware of His presence. You can be at work and totally be aware of His presence. You can also pray in your heart wherever you are. This is about a relationship. It's not about religion. It's about walking with the Holy Spirit of God. It's not a job where you clock in the morning and clock out at night.

It's daily, from the time you rise till you lay your head to sleep.

Remember, God has a way of revealing things to you. Pay attention.
Do you know who the Holy Spirit is?

Do you know how He operates in your life?

Is there a war going on in your heart?

Conclusion It's so important to recognize who the Holy Spirit is. John 16:13 says," However, when He, the Spirit of truth, has come, He will guide you into all truth; for He will not speak on His own authority, but whatever He hears He will speak; and He will tell you things to come." (NKJV) The Holy Spirit dismantles error. John 16:8, "And when He has come, He will convict the world of sin, and righteousness, and of judgement." (NKJV) The Holy Spirit knows the mind of God. So, it's important that we have the mind of Christ. He is our teacher and best friend.

Prayer Dear Lord, we thank you that the devil who has been destroyed, disarmed, defeated and dismantled, no longer has power over us. We thank you that it's not by power or might, but by the Power of your Holy Spirit that we are more than conquers. Amen!

2. Two-edged Sword

There was a young man who thought he held the record for the most trees to be chopped down in his area, but there was an older man who held the record. The young man challenged the older man and the older man agreed. As they began chopping down the trees, the young man noticed the older man would take a fifteen-minute break every hour.

At the end of the day, the young man chopped down six trees, and the older man chopped down eight trees. The young man was furious and threw down his axe and said, how did you chop down more trees than me when you stopped every hour and took a fifteen-minute break?

The older man (gentleman) replied, "I was sharpening my axe.'
Wow! What a powerful story.
Hebrews 4:12 says, "For the word of God is living and powerful, and sharper than any

two-edged sword, piercing even to the division of soul and spirit, and of joints and marrow, and
is a discerner of the thoughts and intents of the heart." (NKJV) If you are spending more time in
the word of God than you are making excuses, welcome to the ten-percentage club!

Remember, the Word brings life, but excuses delay growth.

Are you trying to figure things out your own way?

How much time do you spend sharpening your sword with the Word of God?

Are you tired or feel drained?

Conclusion In times past, before anyone could become a king, he would have to study the book of Proverbs. Proverbs 4:7 says, "Wisdom is the principal thing; therefore, get wisdom. And in your getting, get understanding.'(NKJV) I want to encourage you to read one chapter of Proverbs every day. There are thirty-one chapters, one chapter for each day of the month.

Prayer Father God, I thank you that Your Word is the true Bread of Life that nourishes my soul and gives me strength daily in the mighty name of Jesus. Amen!

3. As a Man Thinketh

It's important that you have faith because your words and mind are very powerful. Job 22:28 says, "You shall decree and declare a thing, and it shall be established for you; so, light will shine on your ways." (NKJV) Proverbs 23:7 says, "For as a man thinks in his heart, so is he. Eat and drink!" he says to you, but his heart is not with you." (NKJV)

Remember, whoever has your mind has you and whoever has your ear, has your future. That's why you need to declare your faith out loud because the Word of God is so powerful. And you can use the Word of God and affirmation throughout the day to strengthen your faith.

There are many powerful scriptures, here are a couple.

Jeremiah 29:11 says, "For I know the thoughts that I think towards you, says the Lord, thoughts of peace and not of evil, to give you a future and a hope." (NKJV)

Psalm 121:1 says, "I will lift my eyes to the hills-from whence comes my help? My help comes from the Lord, who made heaven and earth." (NKJV)

Philippians 4:13 says, "I can do all things through Christ who strengthens me." (NKJV)

Here's an example of an affirmation, I am created for greatness. I have the seed of Almighty God. There's no obstacle that I cannot overcome and there is no disadvantage that can hold me back. I'm in the palm of God's hand. God has equipped and empowered me. The right people are already in my path.

God has released favor into my future. I'm coming into new seasons of increase and abundance. If God be for me, then who can be against me in the name that is above all names, Jesus and I thank you in advance. Remember, be strong enough to ask God for help.

Do you feel like the Bible is boring?

How much time do you spend on social media?

Do you feel like God doesn't hear your prayers?

How much time do you spend watching TV?

Conclusion

Remember to stop giving time to things you don't want to manifest in your life. I want to encourage you to read the Gospels and learn everything about Jesus. He is the One who created you.

Prayer

Dear Lord, I pray to have a hunger for the word and a desire to know you more. To be more aware of your presence and Glory in Jesus mighty name. Amen!

4. A Soldier's Prayer

There was a soldier who just got back from tour. He had been gone for over five years. He stopped by his church one Sunday evening, and to his surprise, no one was there. As he looked through the glass door, he noticed someone inside, it was the janitor. The janitor opened the door and asked the soldier, "How can I help you?"

He replied, "Where is everyone?" The janitor replied, "We no longer have Sunday evening services." If you would like, you're welcome to come and pray in the sanctuary. The soldier was thankful. The janitor even turned on some worship music.

The soldier began to praise and thank God for protecting him, watching over his family and bringing him home safely. To his amazement, he felt the presence of God so powerfully. He asked the Lord, "How is it that your presence is so powerful in here when there is no one here?"
The Lord replied, "It's because no one took Me home with them.

I pray that the love of God is surrounding you right now and may His sweet presence overwhelm you by the Power of the Holy Spirit.

Are you aware of God's presence?

What are you thankful for that God protected you from?

Do you listen to some worship music and just soak in His presence?

Prayer

Father God, let us be aware of your presence, goodness and mercy and let us never take advantage of it in the mighty name of Jesus.

5. Time Management

One morning when I woke up, I went to do my devotions, and I read Ecclesiastes 3. God spoke to me that night about time management. Ecclesiastes 3:1 says, "To everything there is a season, a time for every purpose under heaven." (NKJV). Ecclesiastes 3:8 says, "A time to love, and a time to hate; a time of war, and a time of peace." (NKJV) I said to the Lord, "We're not supposed to hate? Can you give me a revelation on that?

He told me to hate what's happening in the world. To hate that men are not fulfilling their purpose and their destiny. Don't hate the person but hate the sin. There's a righteous hate.
Anger always forces you to focus on the people and things that don't matter. It's good to have a healthy hate but don't hate another person. We are supposed to always love.

Remember, stop wasting your time struggling with things that are not your battles to fight.

What is standing in the way that is keeping you from your purpose and destiny?

What does sin look like to you?

Do you hate lying, lust, worrying or cheating?

Conclusion Remember, God hates sin because it can take you further than you ever thought and keep you longer than you wanted to stay. You must hate whatever has a stronghold on you.

Prayer Father God, help me to hate what you hate, to desire what you desire. Keep me on the street called Straight and let me not compromise my identity in the mighty name of Jesus. Amen!

6. The Luring Wolf

The buffalo is a mighty creature with horns that can cause massive devastation. A wolf knows its limits when he comes around the herd, so he approaches cautiously. He seems harmless when he comes around. The wolf goes straight to the calf. He begins to horse play with the calf until he lures him away from the herd. Once this is accomplished, he devours the calf.

John 10:10 says, "The thief does not come except to steal, and to kill, and to destroy. I have come that they may have life, and that they may have it more abundantly." (NKJV) The devil learns from your mistakes even when you don't.

How do you view sin?

What are some areas in your life where you feel vulnerable?

Why do you think the enemy wants to isolate you?

Are you afraid to ask for prayer?

Conclusion You can call upon the Lord right now.

Prayer Father God, release your supernatural angels to be encamped around me right now and give me strength to get help in the mighty name of Jesus.

7. Let Go

There was a little boy who got his hand stuck in a vase. The mom was frantic because she could not get his hand out. She called 911. The fire department showed up.

They tried warm water and lotion and neither worked. One of the firemen asked the little boy, why did you stick your hand in the vase? The boy replied, "I saw a shiny coin. "He asked," where is the coin? "The boy replied, "in my hand." The fireman told the little boy to let go the coin.

As soon as the little boy opened his hand and released the coin, his hand came out. I believe healing is happening right now as you're reading this. Stop trying to hold onto something that isn't yours. It's time to let go, give it to God and prepare to receive something greater in the mighty name of Jesus.

Do you feel stuck?

Do you feel like your prayers can't get passed the ceiling?

Conclusion The first thing to do is stop feeling sorry for yourself and stop dwelling on the past. Call upon the Lord. He's just one prayer away. Call a friend.

Prayer Father God, thank you that my prayers are breaking out like a waterfall and is bringing healing and peace to everyone around me.

8. Fear Destroys

There was a man that walked into the forest and the tree asked," how many trees are you going to chop down?" He replied, "200 trees with fall this season."

The tree began to whisper to the other trees about the man with the axe. The winds of anxiety began to move throughout the forest. And at the end of the season, 500 trees withered and died.
The young tree asked the older tree," He only cut down 200 trees, but 500 of them passed away. Why did this happen?" The older tree replied, "He said 200 trees would fall, but fear destroyed the other 500."

Fear has kept more people incarcerated than all the prisons of the world. According to 2 Timothy 1:7 "For God has not given us a spirit of fear; but of power and of love and a sound mind." (NKJV)

The only thing you should fear is God and His commandments. They are boundaries that protect us and not harm us. Boundaries don't limit love, they protect it. The less you worry, the more things begin to make sense.

What are your fears?

Do you struggle with anxiety?

My cousin Johnny told me, "Fear is not seeing God in your future. Remember, fear clouds our vision, but God's Word assures us that His presence and promises to extend into tomorrow.

Jeremiah 29:11 says, "For I know the thoughts that I think toward you,

says the Lord, thoughts of
peace and not of evil, to give you a future and a hope." (NKJV)

Do you believe this?

Conclusion
You can worry about it or pray about it. One does nothing. The other does everything.

Prayer
Father God, whatever is crooked you'll make straight. Keep me aligned so I don't get off track, because the safest place to be is in your will.

9. Inventory Your Spiritual Walk

Isn't it ironic that we are more prepared and equipped with our trucks than we are without spiritual walk? We carry all kinds of equipment in our trucks like flashlights, tools, straps, even air compressors- because we might have a flat tire. We carry jumper cables in case somebody is stranded, straps to tow somebody who broke down.

But with our spiritual walk, we often struggle. We even have the most powerful 4x4 which is the Holy Spirit. But the problem is we often allow Him to stay dormant. We need to make an inventory of our gifts and weapons the Lord has given us.

We have all kinds of weapons: prayer, fasting, communion, worship and the Word of God. I challenge you and encourage you to make an inventory of your spiritual walk, because we get out of a rut by getting into a routine. Be rooted in a daily routine and devotion.

What's your favorite scripture?

Who do you go to for prayer?

Do you only pray when you're in trouble?

Do you fast?

What are your spiritual gifts?

Conclusion

You can go to 1 Corinthians 1:7-11 to learn about spiritual gifts. Pray and ask the Lord to reveal which gifts He has placed in your life, so that you may use them to serve others and glorify Him. If you don't have time to pray, then you are busier than God ever intended for you to be.

Prayer

May the Lord give me strength to pray, understanding for His Word and wisdom to walk in the plans He has for me in Jesus' name. Amen!

10. Your Identity in Christ

It is important to know your identity in the Lord and to embrace the assignment He has given you. You must know what your passion is, for it often reveals the direction of your calling.

Philippians 3:10 says," that I may know Him and the power of His resurrection, and the fellowship of His sufferings, being conformed to His death." (NKJV) So, when you go to church, you won't be moved by what happens there because you know God has called you to be there for His purpose and glory. You were born to help someone overcome the darkest season of their life.

Acts 20:35, "I have shown you in every way, by laboring like this, that you must support the weak. And remember the words of the Lord Jesus, that He said, 'It is more blessed to give that to receive." (NKJV) So now when you go to church, you will have a different mindset.

You will want to give your time and talents, even outside the church like your community. You will want to give your praise and worship, offering your heart fully to the Lord in gratitude and reverence. You will want to give whatever God entrusted to you. It doesn't matter if the church seems to be in chaos; perhaps God has placed you there to help rebuild it with love and reverence for Him.

To pray for and help heal the church, is to stand as a vessel of God's restoration, it is to seek His presence until the fire of the Holy Spirit is rekindled, bringing renewal, unity, and strength back
to the body of Christ. This is a powerful revelation. Too many are looking for an excuse to leave. An excuse is a well-planned, planned lie.

Now if God tells you to leave, you leave. I understand there are certain situations where you must leave a church. I believe God will give you the release and peace to leave.

Why is it important to know your purpose?

Have you forgiven them?

Has a church hurt you?

Conclusion
It's important to know your identity in Christ because that is your anchor when offenses come and they will come.
God never said trust man. He said to trust Him and love man. In the middle of the Bible, in
Psalm 118:8 it says, "It is better to trust in the Lord than to put confidence in man." (NKJV)

Prayer
May God put a fire in your belly and may you be a walking torch to a dark world. May your fire beso contagious that it flames the identity of Christ to those around you with breath and power ofHis Holy Spirit.

11. The Enemy Waits

1 Corinthians 16:9 says, "for a great and effective door has opened to me and there are many adversaries." (NKJV) Now you understand why it feels as though an enemy stands against you.

Maybe you keep battling and nothing seems to work for you, but if you read the context, it says there's an enemy standing at the door. He is studying you, and I am sure he has already taken inventory of your weaknesses.

He knows your strengths and weaknesses. Ephesians 4:27 says, "nor give place to the devil." (NKJV) He will lie to anyone who will listen. Do not believe anything he says about your past or future.

James 4:7 says, "Therefore submit to God. Resist the devil and he will flee from you." (NKJV) You do not have to fear what is in front of you when you know who is walking right beside you. remember to be thankful for the doors that are closed, detours and roadblocks, because they
often protect you from plans not meant for you. When God opens the next door, you are going to understand why the enemy fought you so hard.

What do you feel like your weaknesses are?

Do you feel like the enemy has been accusing you or using you?

Do you feel restless?

Conclusion

Remember, the battles don't belong to you, they belong to the Lord. If you have been fighting in the flesh, you will lose every time. These are spiritual battles to be fought on your knees in prayer.

Prayer

Father God, may I get a hold of the Word of God, and may I know that enemies are doorways to my next blessing in the mighty name of Jesus.

12. Don't Throw in the Towel

There was a young boy who told his father that he wanted to quit school. He said he was tired and frustrated and that school was meaningless. His father replied, "do you know who Abraham Lincoln is?" The son replied, "well yes."

The father asked, "what about Daryl Kenner?" The son replied, "I don't know who he is." The father replied, "No one will know who you are if you quit right now. I want to encourage you: you've come a long way, and sometimes you may feel like giving up, remember that your breakthrough is right around the corner.

You've come too far to throw in the towel. Your promotion is coming, your marriage is becoming stronger, and your children are coming back to the Lord. Appreciate where you are right now, because you have come a long way. And don't expect people to always do what is best for you, that is your responsibility. I pray that you will not make decisions when you are feeling tired, frustrated, or anxious.

Do you feel frustrated?

Have you lost your focus or motivation?

Conclusion

If you focus on your problems you'll create stress, but if you focus on your solutions, you'll create peace and leverage.

What are some solutions to create peace?

Prayer
Father God, renew my focus, strength, discipline and desire. Keep my mind stayed on you in the mighty name of Jesus. Amen!

13. Turn off the Phone

I remember taking my son, Austin, fishing when he was eight years old. We went to this place called, The Log Jam. As we began to fish, my phone kept ringing. Customers were calling and were wanting an estimate for stain concrete.

As I turned to my right, I noticed Austin shrugging his shoulders. I realized at that moment what was important. I turned my phone off and put it away. I looked over at Austin and said, "you are more important than the phone -or the business it carries)."
We didn't catch a lot of fish, but we made some great memories. Being a father is not about trying to be a superhero-it's about being there and being present.

A text can never replace showing up in person. Presence is powerful. Maybe your dad wasn't there when you were young, but now that you're older, your children long for you to be present in their lives.
I just want to encourage you: you can't change the past, but you can change the future.

Children's Love language is time, and time is precious. Time is not refundable, so be mindful of what you spend it on. Spending time with your family is important, but most important is spending time with the (Heavenly) Father. He is ever present with you, and longs to hear from you. Stop right now and just begin to thank Him for all that He's done for you.

What's important to you?

How do you define quality time?

Whoever (or what) gets most of your time is important to you?

Conclusion
Remember, spending time with God and family is never a waste of time

Prayer
Father God, we come to You asking You to teach us to number our days, to be wise with our time, and to make the best of every moment in the mighty name of Jesus. Amen!

14. Lack of Discipline

In these times we are living in right now, we are missing the fear of the Lord.

Proverbs 1:7 says, "The fear of the Lord is the beginning of knowledge, but fools despise wisdom and instruction." (NKJV) and if you read Hosea 4:6 it says, my people are destroyed for lack of knowledge. Because you have rejected knowledge, I also will reject you from being priest for Me; because you have forgotten the law of your God, I also will forget your children." (NKJV)

They both go hand in hand. It is the fear of the Lord that protects and guard you. Hebrews 12:6 says," For whom the Lord loves He chastens, and scourges every son whom He receives." (NKJV) If you don't receive any discipline, then He may not know you.

Do you feel convicted when you watch porn, lust or lie? If you have, that's a good sign that the Holy Spirit is convicting you. It's God telling you that this path will cause harm.

If you don't stop, it will become a stronghold and it will eventually destroy you. Sin doesn't just affect you, but everyone around you. Sooner or later, we must step out of the storm we created, because broken people break people

Being aware of your poisonous behavior is the first step into fixing it.

Why do you think porn, lust or lying will harm you?

Do you believe it will affect people around you?

Do you want to surrender these strongholds to God?

What are some actions you can take to start walking in freedom?

Prayer
Father God, we declare every stronghold to be broken and uprooted in the name of Jesus and chains will begin to fall and minds will begin to be set free.

15. Affective Prayer with the Word

Sometimes we forget that prayer is so powerful, and that it moves the hand of God. It is a very powerful weapon that we are not applying much in our lives. I don't mean long prayers, but short and effective prayers that come directly from the Word of God. Remember if you pray for change, prepare for challenges.

Allow the Holy Spirit to teach you how to pray just by asking and listening. You will become strategic on how to pray. Then, begin to start writing the prayers down, so they will become a record of your faith and a reminder of God's answers.

Here's an example:
Father God, move mightily through my business, help me to make wise decisions according to Proverbs 3:5-6 says, Trust in the Lord with all your heart, and lean not on your own understanding; in all your ways acknowledge Him, and He shall direct your paths." (NKJV) I thank you, Lord, for giving me discernment in the mighty name of Jesus. Amen!

Your faith will fight for you if you let it, and may God give you wisdom for every decision.

List three events that impacted you negatively:

1.

2.

3.

Now look back on what you learned from it and how you overcame it. Romans 8:28 says, "And we know that all things work together for good for those who love God and are called according to His purpose." (NKJV) Just because you made a bad decision doesn't mean you're going to have a bad life. God redeems mistakes and gives new beginnings.

Learn from your mistakes and don't let them define you. Remember that mistake you made three years ago? Nobody else did either, so let it go. You will become wiser, better and stronger. Be a bridge for others who are lost, guiding them in truth.

You will grow from this lesson, so don't give so much energy to things you can't control. Instead, trust God with what is beyond your reach.

Conclusion

God is waiting for you. He is already battling the things you've been wrestling with.

Prayer

Lord, I thank you that I can rest knowing that I don't have to carry it anymore in the might name of Jesus.

16. A Compass

One night, I had a dream in which I saw a crocodile swimming after two men in the water, while the people were screaming. No one was helping to scare off the crocodile or to rescue the men. I became angry because people were just standing there. I ran to help, but suddenly the crocodile turned into an anaconda and began to swallow the men.
I pulled the men out and began to step on the anaconda's head, but it was gone. I woke up and I realized that the devil has been defeated and dismantled, but he is striking fear in so many people these days. The Lord is calling me to write this book to help people who are drowning spiritually, offering them hope, guidance, and a way back to His presence.
The enemy wants you to believe you are the only one going through this, but you're not. Struggling doesn't mean failing, it means you're still pressing forward. So, press on. Remember, this book is not meant to replace the Word of God. It is simply a compass, pointing people back to Him.

What are your reasons to live?

What are some battles that no one knows about?

List some things you can't change.

Conclusion

Begin to focus on the things you can change. Remember, God never changes, and neither does His Word. He will never leave you nor forsake you, for his presence is constant and His promises are true.

Prayer

Father God, according to Matthew 11-30 says, "For My yoke is easy and My burden is light." (NKJV)I can rest in the assurance that Your love for me is constant, unchanging, and faithful.

17. Times of Frustration

Mother's Day was coming up, and the father told his son that they were going to get a gift for the boy's mom. He told his son that we needed to go to the store, and not to wander off to look at toys. As they began shopping the father was looking at some cards when he noticed that his son was gone. The father began to walk down the aisles, and there he was, playing with a toy gun. The father told his son, "Let's go home with a stern voice." The young boy knew he was in trouble.

When they got home, the father told him to go straight to his room without supper. The mother asked, "What was wrong and what did he do?" The father replied, "he just doesn't listen." So later that evening the little boy knocked on the door and the father said, "I told you to stay in your." An hour later the boy knocked on the door again and the father said, "you better have a good reason for knocking on the door?"

The little boy responded, "I wanted to know if we were still friends?" At that moment the father realized what he had done. He had been stressed all week because work was slow and he was hitting a financial barrier.

He took his frustration out on his son. Is there a time when you were frustrated and you kept it in, or did you take your frustration out on someone close to you? Maybe your dad did that to you? Don't allow your pain to develop a personality. Pain is a wakeup call. It's notifying you that something must change.

Who hurt you?

What are some things that you're holding onto?

Conclusion

Ask God to help you let go of things that you've been holding onto. It's time to let go of the pain of your past. Let the healing begin in the mighty name of Jesus. I don't know what they did to you, but I know what God did for you. I pray as you are reading this that the pain of your past is being released right now in the mighty name of Jesus.

Prayer

Dear Lord, expose any darkness that has been hindering my walk with you. I release any pain of my past, because there is power in forgiveness in the name of Jesus. Amen!

18. Financial Inventory

Proverbs 27:23 says, "Be diligent to know the state of your flock and attend to your herds." This is very important because we need to keep track of our financial inventory. We need to be aware of where it's coming and where it's going out. By keeping track, you gain clarity on where provision comes from and how it is being used.

Seventy-five percent of divorces happen because of finances. Do you check your bank accounts daily? Do you have a budget? Does being in debt make you feel angry or depressed? Money is not evil; it is the love of money that is evil. Money is just a tool. It gives you freedom when you're a good steward with it. I want to encourage you to find a financial mentor or take some classes on wealth.

The Bible also teaches us about giving, and these principles are not negotiable. God is not trying to take something from you; rather, He desires to bless and shape you into a faithful steward of His resources.
If you're struggling with money or giving, ask God right now to help you and teach you. May the Lord give you financial wisdom and people around to help guide you to become fruitful in all that you do.

Are you constantly chasing money?

Do you struggle with making decisions with marriage, finances, or your children?

When you come home, is it chaos?

Is love the foundation of your home?

Can you describe love?

Are you empty inside?

Have you lost your first love?

Prayer

Father God, we love you because you first loved us. I can't know love until I know you. I receive your love right now and I thank you for filling every void place in my life now in the might name of Jesus. Amen!

19. Grace

There was a young man walking along the road and smoking a joint. Suddenly, a cowboy riding his horse stopped beside him and asked, "Son, how are you doing?" The young man replied, "I'm okay. But I was curious, what is the name of your horse?" The cowboy smiled and said, "His name is Grace."

Before the cowboy rode off, he looked at the young man and said, "Remember this, Jesus loves you". As time passed, the young man often thought back to that moment. He thought "I want to thank the cowboy for planting a seed in my life." He found later that the cowboy was living in a nursing home.

He walked into the nursing home and went over to the cowboy. With hope in his voice, he said, "Do you remember me?" The cowboy replied,' Yes, and Jesus loves you." The young man began to cry and told him, "Thank you."

You didn't condemn me and didn't even tell me to stop smoking marijuana. You had no idea what I was going through and how much I blamed and hated God.

Later, I gave my life to the Lord. He asked, "How was Grace the horse doing?" The cowboy replied, "Grace passed away many years ago. But listen, grace carried me this far, and now grace will carry you all the way to Glory Land."

"I feel the presence of God all over you right now, and I thank God for His grace that is carrying you this very moment." No matter how deep you have sunk into depression or have strayed away, His love will find you, and His grace will deliver you

Do you ever feel like you're going in circles?

Have you truly submitted to God?

Have you fully surrendered to His will?

Like your prayers are not being answered?

Conclusion

Jesus said in Luke 22:24" Father, if it is Your will, take this cup away from Me; nevertheless, not My will, but Yours, be done." (NKJV) It's not that you don't know what to do, it's that you don't like your choices.

Prayer

Father God, I pray that I truly surrender to your will. You are Lord over my relationships, finances and my life. Help me to die daily of this flesh and to work out my salvation with fear and trembling in the mighty name of Jesus. Amen!

20. Dirt or Diamonds

There was a married couple who went on a retreat in Arkansas to sift diamonds. As they began to sift for diamonds, the husband kept finding only dirt, while the wife discovered small shavings of diamonds and celebrated each one.

Frustrated, the husband grew angry and threw down his bowl.
He cried out to the Lord, "Why does she keep getting diamonds and I only get dirt?" The Lord answered, "It's because you keep looking for the dirt in her, and not the diamonds."

The husband fell on his knees and began to weep. And perhaps the same is true for us, we often keep looking for the dirt in people, and not the diamonds. We are all flawed, but that is what makes us beautiful. Whatever you are looking for is also looking for you.

If you're looking for the dirt in someone, you'll surely find it. But if you're looking for beauty in someone, you'll find that too. What are you looking for? Remember, when you throw dirt, you lose ground.

Do you have unforgiveness?

"But if you do not forgive men their trespasses, neither will your Father forgive your trespasses." Matthew 6-15 (NKJV)
"If anyone says," I love God," and hates his brother, he is a liar; for he does not love his brother whom he has seen, how can he love God whom he has not seen? 1 John 4:20 (NKJV)

Are you angry at your spouse?

Conclusion

"Husbands, likewise, dwell with them with understanding, giving honor to the wife, as to the weaker vessel, and as being heirs together of the grace of life, that your prayers may not be hindered." 1 Peter 3-7 (NKJV) Just because someone is strong enough to handle pain, doesn't mean they deserve it.

Prayer

Father God, You're the Rock I want to build my foundation on. Fill me with Your love daily so I can truly love others and walk in total victory every day in the mighty name of Jesus.

21. The Foundation of Love

A young boy was being raised by his grandparents. One day his grandfather came home and saw three men standing outside. Curious, he asked who they were. The grandmother stepped outside and said, "These three men are Love, Wisdom, and Wealth. But we can only invite one of them into our home. The grandfather said, "Well that's easy.

We need wealth, because money has been tight all year long." The grandmother spoke gently, "We need wisdom, because we have been making bad decisions lately." As the grandparents argued, the little boy began to cry. Through his tears he said, "We need love." So, they invited Love into their home.

As soon as Love entered the home, Wisdom and Wealth followed also. The grandfather was puzzled and said, "I thought only one of you were welcomed in our home?" Love responded, "' Wherever Love goes, Wisdom and Wealth follow".

The moment we begin to love and forgive, our life will shift into a new beginning. Love is perfect. It's just the people we love aren't. When we love someone, we carry more thread and needle than we do scissors.

It's important that we make an inventory of our heart. Is your heart lined up to God's will?

Is there any bitterness in your heart?

Is there anyone you haven't forgiven?

Is there someone who passed away and they still have a stronghold in your life?

Conclusion

Please stop right now and ask the Holy Spirit to help forgive whoever hurt you and to help heal your heart. It's important that you have love as your foundation. Matthew 22-37 says, "Jesus said to Him, "You shall love the Lord your God with all your heart, with all your soul, and with all your mind." (NKJV) **Matthew 22:39** says, "And the second is like it: 'You shall love your neighbors as yourself." (NKJV)

Have you forgiven yourself?

If you want to know what's in your heart, listen to your mouth.

Prayer

Father God, we thank You that Your Blood breaks every chain, curse and stronghold. I release any bitterness towards anyone and ask You to fill me with your unconditional love in Jesus' name.

22. Clogged Heart

I came home one day and noticed our sink was clogged. I let my wife, Leslie, know that I needed to fix it. She suggested, "Why don't you use liquid Drano to unclog it?" I replied, "I'm just going to remove the T-trap underneath the sink and unclog it myself."

She said, "Okay." So, I began to work underneath the sink, but I realized I didn't have the right tool. Now I'm frustrated. So, we went to Home Depot to buy the tool I needed. As I began to remove the T-trap, water came down and splashed all over me.

Now I'm really agitated but also relieved that it came off. I made sure the T- trap was clean, and I put it back underneath the sink. I began to run the faucet, and it clogged up again. I grabbed the liquid Drano and poured it into the sink, and just like that, it was fixed. My goodness, all I had to do was listen to my wife, but I had too much pride.

I'm so thankful for my wife because she is so patient and loving. I now consider myself a first responder because when she calls, I respond.

Are you thankful for your spouse?

How often do you say I love you and I'm thankful for you?

Do you know your spouse's love language?

Do y'all hold hands and pray together?

Prayer
Father God, I thank You for giving me wisdom, understanding, a listening ear, love, and grace for my marriage. May I never take it for granted in the mighty name of Jesus.

23. In All Things Give Thanks

Psalms 95:2 says "Let us come before His presence with thanksgiving; Let us shout joyfully to Him with psalms." (NKJV) I just want to encourage you to thank God for who He is and for what He has done in your life. He is the Great I Am, the King of kings and Lord of Lords. Thank Him for waking you up, and for giving you another day.

Thank Him for your family and friends. After you thank Him, be still and learn to listen to the voice of the Holy Spirit. After that, you can begin to make your supplications known to the Lord. According to Philippian's 4:6-7 "Be anxious for nothing, but in everything by prayer and supplication, with thanksgiving, let your requests be made known to God; and the peace of God which surpasses all understanding, will guard your hearts and minds through Christ Jesus." (NKJV)

Sometimes we make prayers so difficult. We think that if our prayers aren't long, God won't hear us. But that is a lie from the pit of hell.

Matthew 6:6 says, "But when you pray, go into your room, and when you have shut the door, pray to your Father who is in the secret place; and your Father who sees in secret will reward you openly." (NKJV) It's not about how long or short your prayers are.

It's about a relationship and learning to hear from God and being obedient to His voice.

How much time do you spend with God?

What are you thankful for?

Do you listen to the voice of the Holy Spirit?

Do you get distracted?

Conclusion I would like to encourage you to have a paper and pen next to you and write down the plans you have for the day, so you don't get distracted when you pray.

Your alone time is for everyone's benefit.

Prayer Father God, help to keep my mind stayed on You, to be sensitive to the voice of the Holy Spirit and to learn to be still and know that You are God.

Scripture Reference List (NKJV)

Psalms
Psalm 119:164 – "Seven times a day I praise You…"
Psalm 121:1–2 – "I will lift up mine eyes unto the hills…" Psalm 118:8 – "It is better to trust in the Lord…"
Psalm 95:2 – "Let us come before his presence with thanksgiving…"

John
John 16:13 – "When he, the Spirit of truth, is come, he will guide you…" John 16:8 – "And when he is come, he will reprove the world of sin…" John 10:10 – "The thief cometh not, but for to steal…

Hebrews
Hebrews 4:12 – "For the word of God is quick, and powerful…" Hebrews 12:6 – "For whom the Lord loveth he chasteness…"

Proverbs
Proverbs 4:7 – "Wisdom is the principal thing…"
Proverbs 23:7 – "For as he thinketh in his heart, so is he."
Proverbs 1:7 – "The fear of the Lord is the beginning of knowledge…"

Proverbs 27:23 – "Be Thou diligent to know the state of thy flocks…"

Job

Job 22:28 – "Thou shalt also decree a thing…"

Jeremiah

Jeremiah 29:11 – "For I know the thoughts that I think toward you…"

Philippians

Philippians 4:13 – "I can do all things through Christ…"
Philippians 4:6–7 – "Be anxious for nothing; but in everything by prayer…"

Ecclesiastes

Ecclesiastes 3:1 – "To everything there is a season…" Ecclesiastes 3:8 – "A time to love, and a time to hate…"

---

1 Corinthians

1 Corinthians 1:7–11 – (Spiritual gifts) 1 Corinthians 16:9 – "For a great door and effectual is opened unto me…"

Ephesians

Ephesians 4:27 – "Neither give place to the devil."

James
James 4:7 – "Submit yourselves therefore to God…"

2 Timothy
2 Timothy 1:7 – "For God hath not given us the spirit of fear…"

Acts
Acts 20:35 – "It is more blessed to give than to receive."

Matthew
Matthew 6:6 – "When thou pray, enter into thy closet…"
Matthew 6:15 – "If ye forgive not men their trespasses…"
Matthew 22:37 – "Thou shalt love the Lord thy God…"
Matthew 22:39 – "Thou shalt love thy neighbor as thyself."
Matthew 11:30 – "For my yoke is easy…"

1 John
1 John 4:20 – "If a man say, I love God, and hates his brother…"

Luke
Luke 22:42 – "Not my will, but thine, be done."

Romans

Romans 8:28 – "All things work together for good…"

---

1 Peter

1 Peter 3:7 – "Giving honor unto the wife…"

Hosea

Hosea 4:6 – "My people are destroyed for lack of knowledge…"

Flo Vasquez is a devoted husband to Leslie Vasquez and a passionate servant of God. He enjoys singing, writing, and using the gifts the Lord has entrusted to him. With a heart for reaching the lost and a calling to help men discover their identity in Christ, Flo's life and ministry are centered on restoration and spiritual growth. His book, The Inventory, was born out of his passion-a desire to guide readers in examining their lives, releasing what no longer serve them, and embracing the treasures of grace and purpose found in God's presence. Through his words, Flo invites men and women alike to take inventory of their spiritual journey and to embrace their identity that Christ has prepared for them.

Conclusion

I pray that this book encourages and challenges you. I hope this book helped to draw you closer to the Lord. I pray you will share your testimony of how God used this book to help you take a closer look at your life. My hope is that this book can be a compass to point someone back to the Lord and His word. If you haven't received Christ as your Lord and Savior, you can say this prayer right now.

According to Romans 10:9 it says, "That if you confess with your mouth the Lord Jesus and believe in your heart that God has raised Him from the dead, you will be saved." (NKJV) If you said that prayer, and received Christ in your heart, welcome to the family. The following page has a certificate for you to put your name on. It is a reminder that your name is written in "the Lamb's book of Life." Remember, it's a daily walk, not a marathon.

CERTIFICATE
OF DEDICATION

THIS CERTIFIES THAT

_____

HAS CONFESSED HIS/HER FAITH IN N
JESUS CHRIST AND IS NOW A
DISCIPLE OF THE LORD.

| DATE | PASTOR'S SIGNATURE |

Inventory Page

As you begin to do an inventory of your life

Made in the USA
Coppell, TX
30 December 2025

67564300R00035